Olympic Hero
Pro Wrestler
Kurt Angle

by A. R. Schaefer

Reading Consultant:
Dr. Robert Miller
Professor of Special Education
Minnesota State University, Mankato

CAPSTONE
HIGH-INTEREST
BOOKS

an imprint of Capstone Press
Mankato, Minnesota

D1291995

Capstone High-Interest Books are published by Capstone Press
151 Good Counsel Drive, P.O. Box 669, Mankato, Minnesota 56002
www.capstonepress.com

Library of Congress Cataloging-in-Publication Data
Schaefer, Adam.
Olympic hero: pro wrestler Kurt Angle/by A.R. Schaefer.
    v. cm.—(Pro wrestlers)
    Includes bibliographical references (p. 45) and index.
    Contents: WWF champion—The early years—Olympic champion—WWF
star—Kurt Angle today.
    ISBN 0-7368-1310-1 (hardcover)
    1. Angle, Kurt—Juvenile literature. 2. Wrestlers—United States—Biography—
Juvenile literature. [1. Angle, Kurt. 2. Wrestlers.]
I. Title. II. Series.
GV1196.A55 S32 2003
796.812'092—dc21   2001007719

Summary: Traces the life and career of amateur and pro wrestler Kurt Angle.

Editorial Credits
Angela Kaelberer, editor; Karen Risch, product planning editor; Timothy Halldin,
    series designer; Gene Bentdahl, book designer; Jo Miller, photo researcher

Photo Credits
AP/Wide World Photos, 12, 15, 41
Dr. Michael Lano, cover (all), 4, 6, 10, 29, 33, 37, 38, 42
Glenn Cratty/Getty Images, 17
Jed Jacobsohn/Getty Images, 18, 22, 26
Rich Freeda/WWF Entertainment via Getty Images, 30
Szenes/CORBIS SYGMA, 34
TempSport/CORBIS, 24
Tom G. Lynn/Timepix, 21

J
92
Angle

2 3 4 5 6 7 11 10 09 08 07 06

Capstone Press thanks Dr. Michael Lano, WReaLano@aol.com, for his assistance in
the preparation of this book.

Table of Contents

Chapter 1

WWF Champion

On October 22, 2000, professional wrestling fans gathered at the Pepsi Arena in Albany, New York. The fans were there for the World Wrestling Federation (WWF)'s No Mercy event.

Kurt Angle entered the arena to face Dwayne Johnson for the last match of the night. Johnson wrestles as The Rock. The Rock was the WWF World Champion. Kurt would become the champion if he defeated The Rock.

Early Advantage

Kurt walked to the ring with Stephanie McMahon. Stephanie was Kurt's manager.

Kurt and The Rock battled both inside and outside of the ring. Kurt climbed to the top rope

Kurt hoped to become the WWF World Champion.

Kurt wrestled The Rock for the WWF Championship.

and tried to land a moonsault on The Rock. Kurt did a backward somersault off the top rope. The Rock moved out of the way. The Rock then hit Kurt with a DDT. For this move, he put Kurt into a front facelock and fell straight down as he drove Kurt's head into the mat.

Stephanie stood over Kurt to protect him from The Rock. The Rock took her down with a Rock

Bottom. For this move, he wrapped his arm around Stephanie's head and neck. He picked her up and slammed her to the mat. Kurt then got up and clotheslined The Rock.

Outside Interference

Paul Levesque ran into the ring. Levesque wrestles as Triple H. Triple H punched Kurt and took The Rock down with a Pedigree. Triple H held The Rock face down. The Rock's head was locked between his legs. Triple H dropped to his knees as he slammed The Rock's head to the mat. Triple H then carried Stephanie out of the ring.

Kurt tried to cover The Rock for the pin. But The Rock kicked out after two counts. The wrestlers both jumped out of the ring.

Solofa Fatu came out to help The Rock. Fatu wrestles as Rikishi. Rikishi hit Kurt and threw him back into the ring. The Rock followed and took Kurt down with a Rock Bottom. The Rock covered Kurt for the pin, but Kurt kicked out. Rikishi got into the ring and charged toward Kurt. At the last second, Kurt moved out of Rikishi's way. Rikishi hit The Rock instead.

Kurt finished off both wrestlers with one of his signature moves, the Angle Slam. Kurt picked up Rikishi. He slammed Rikishi's back to the mat. He then took down The Rock. The referee counted to three. Kurt was the WWF World Champion.

About Kurt Angle

Kurt Angle is 6 feet, 2 inches (188 centimeters) tall and weighs 220 pounds (100 kilograms). Kurt was a great amateur wrestler before he became a pro wrestler. He won a gold medal at the 1996 Olympic Games in Atlanta, Georgia.

Kurt began his professional wrestling career in 1998. He joined the WWF in September 1999. Since then, he has won the WWF World Championship twice. He also has held the WWF European, Intercontinental, and Hardcore titles.

In March 2001, the WWF bought World Championship Wrestling (WCW). That wrestling company was located in Atlanta. After the sale, Kurt won the WCW U.S. Championship and the WCW World Championship.

Major Matches

November 14, 1999—Kurt defeats Shawn Stasiak at Survivor Series to win his first TV match.

February 8, 2000—Kurt defeats Val Venis to win the WWF European Championship.

February 27, 2000—Kurt defeats Chris Jericho to win the WWF Intercontinental Championship.

June 25, 2000—Kurt defeats Rikishi to win the King of the Ring Tournament.

October 22, 2000—Kurt defeats The Rock to win his first WWF World Championship.

July 24, 2001—Kurt defeats Booker T to win the WCW World Championship.

September 10, 2001—Kurt defeats Rob Van Dam to win the WWF Hardcore Championship.

September 23, 2001—Kurt defeats Steve Austin to win his second WWF World Championship.

October 22, 2001—Kurt defeats Rhyno to win the WCW U.S. Championship.

Chapter 2

The Early Years

Kurt Angle was born December 9, 1968, in Pittsburgh, Pennsylvania. His father's name was David. His mother is Jackie. Kurt has four older brothers and one older sister. His brothers are David, Mark, Johnny, and Eric. His sister is Le'Anne.

Kurt grew up in Dormont, Pennsylvania. This city is near Pittsburgh. Kurt's father worked as a crane operator for a construction company. His mother was a secretary.

High School Athlete

Sports were important to the Angle family. All of Kurt's brothers were good athletes in high

Kurt was born December 9, 1968.

11

Kurt became interested in wrestling at a young age.

school. The entire family attended as many of the boys' sporting events as possible.

Kurt's family moved to Mount Lebanon, Pennsylvania, when he was in sixth grade. Kurt played football and wrestled at Mount Lebanon High School. Kurt enjoyed playing football. But he liked the challenge of wrestling even more.

A Big Loss

Kurt's father never missed any of Kurt's sporting events. David Angle often told people that Kurt would grow up to be the best athlete in the family.

In August 1985, David fell off a crane at a construction site. He landed on his head and cracked his skull. David died in a hospital two days later.

Kurt was only 16 when his father died. David's death was very hard for Kurt. Kurt wanted to make his father's dream come true. He decided he would work even harder at becoming a great athlete.

Kurt's first football game of the season was later that week. He played one of the best games of his life. Kurt recovered two fumbles, scored two touchdowns, and made 16 tackles in the game to help Mount Lebanon win.

Top Athlete

Kurt's athletic skills continued to improve. In 11th grade, he placed third in the heavyweight class at the Pennsylvania AAA Interscholastic Athletic Association championships.

In 12th grade, Kurt did even better at sports. He was the Pennsylvania heavyweight wrestling champion. The same year, he won the Junior National Freestyle tournament in the heavyweight division. He also was named the football Defensive Player of the Year for western Pennsylvania.

College Wrestler

Kurt graduated from Mount Lebanon in 1987. He wanted to continue playing sports in college. He had to decide between football and wrestling. A few colleges wanted Kurt to play football for them. But most college football coaches thought he was too small. At the time, Kurt was 5 feet, 10 inches (178 centimeters) tall and weighed about 200 pounds (91 kilograms).

Kurt decided to attend Clarion University in Clarion, Pennsylvania. This small college has a strong wrestling program. Kurt did well during his first year at Clarion. He won 29 matches. He also was named the Pennsylvania State Athletic Conference (PSAC) Freshman of the Year.

Kurt's goal in college was to wrestle in the Olympics.

The next year, Kurt skipped the wrestling season. He spent the season lifting weights and training. He thought the extra training would help him win a national championship.

Kurt's training paid off during the 1990 season. He had a 30-0-1 record during the regular season. He hurt his knee four days before the NCAA championships. But he still won the NCAA Division I heavyweight title.

Another Championship

Kurt had another great season in 1991. He won 33 matches in a row. He then hurt his knee about one month before the NCAA championships. Kurt still wrestled at the tournament, but he lost his final match.

Kurt was disappointed with his second-place finish. He wanted to win one more national championship before he graduated. Kurt trained hard before the 1992 season began. He took a 26-0 record into the NCAA championships.

In his last match, Kurt's opponent was Sylvester Terkay from North Carolina State University. Kurt weighed 199 pounds (90 kilograms). Terkay weighed 275 pounds (125 kilograms). But Kurt defeated Terkay to win his second NCAA title.

In 1992, Kurt graduated from Clarion with a degree in geography. At Clarion, Kurt won 116 matches, lost 10, and tied two. He also set several school records. His records for 150 single-season takedowns and 355 career takedowns still stand.

Kurt Angle's Hero: Bruce Baumgartner

Kurt respected many top athletes as he grew up. One of his biggest heroes was champion heavyweight wrestler Bruce Baumgartner. Baumgartner wrestled for Indiana State University and won an NCAA championship in 1982. He was the world champion in 1986, 1993, and 1995. He won Olympic gold medals in 1984 and 1992.

Baumgartner's career record is 134-12. He holds several U.S. wrestling records. These records include most Olympic medals, most world champion medals, and most national titles. He was the national freestyle champion each year between 1980 and 1996.

In 1996, Baumgartner and Kurt were Olympic teammates. Baumgartner won a bronze medal.

Chapter 3

Olympic Champion

Kurt began training with the U.S. wrestling team right after college. In 1992, he finished third at the World Cup championships and fourth at the U.S. Nationals. Later that year, he tried out for the U.S. Olympic team. But he did not make the team.

Improving Skills

Kurt was disappointed when he did not make the Olympic team. But he wrestled well in 1993. He finished second at the U.S. Nationals. He also won the Henri Deglane Challenge in France.

Kurt was disappointed when he did not make the Olympic team in 1992.

In 1994, Kurt finished second at the U.S. Nationals and the World Team Trials. He also became the fourth U.S. wrestler to win a gold medal at the Krasnoyarsk Tournament in Siberia, Russia.

Kurt continued to do well in 1995. He was the World Team Trials champion. He also won the U.S. Nationals and the Grand Prix Slovakia. He finished second in the World Cup championships.

Chance at the Pros

In 1995, Kurt had an opportunity to play professional football. The Pittsburgh Steelers asked Kurt to try out for their team. The Steelers are Kurt's favorite football team. His family often watched the Steelers' games on TV when Kurt was growing up.

Kurt practiced for the Steelers in February 1995. He thought his tryout went well except in one area. Kurt was not able to run very fast on the field. The Steelers did not offer him a contract.

Kurt trained hard to make the 1996 Olympic team.

Training for a Dream

Kurt wanted to make the Olympic team in 1996. He began training even harder.

Kurt trained seven hours each day. He began his day by riding an exercise bike to warm up. He followed the bike ride with a 4-mile (6.4-kilometer) run. He then carried a wrestling partner up a 200-yard (183-meter)

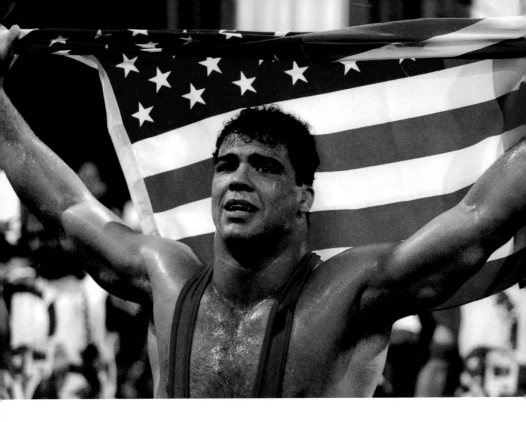

Kurt qualified for the 1996 Olympic wrestling team.

hill about 15 times. Kurt's wrestling partner
weighed about 185 pounds (84 kilograms). In
the afternoon, Kurt wrestled against other
wrestlers. In the evening, he lifted weights.
He tried to lift the weights until he could
not lift anymore. Each week, he added
more weight. Once, he lifted 225 pounds

(102 kilograms) 77 times. The next week, he lifted 315 pounds (143 kilograms) 41 times.

An Injury

Kurt's training schedule improved his wrestling in 1996. He again won the U.S. Nationals. He qualified for the U.S. Olympic team in the 220-pound (100-kilogram) weight class.

During Nationals, Kurt cracked two bones in his back and pulled four muscles in his neck. Two of the disks in his back were out of place. The injury made wrestling both painful and dangerous. Doctors told Kurt he had to stop wrestling. Wrestling while injured could have left him unable to walk. But Kurt did not want to stop.

Another doctor gave Kurt shots of a strong painkiller in his neck before his matches. These shots kept Kurt from feeling pain as he wrestled. Today, Kurt says he realizes what he did was very dangerous. But at the time, all Kurt could think about was winning the gold medal.

The Olympics

At the Olympics, Kurt won his first four
matches to make it into the finals. He faced
Abbas Jadidi of Iran for the gold medal.

The match was close. Neither wrestler
scored until late in the match. Jadidi turned
Kurt and earned one point. Kurt scored a
takedown 25 seconds later to tie the score at
1-1. Neither wrestler scored again.

To break a tie, referees first look at the
number of cautions. Referees caution the
wrestlers when they break the rules. Both Kurt
and Jadidi had two cautions. The tie meant the
referees had to vote for a winner.

Kurt and Jadidi waited in the ring for
several minutes for the referees' decision.
Then, a referee held up Kurt's hand. Kurt
had won the match and the gold medal.

Kurt cried as he fell to his knees. He had
achieved his goal. He was one of the best
wrestlers in the world.

Kurt fell to his knees after winning the gold medal.

Chapter 4

WWF Star

After the Olympics, Kurt received much attention from the public. People in Pittsburgh held parades in his honor. He appeared on TV talk shows. He even met President Bill Clinton.

After the Olympics

For about six months, Kurt traveled the country and gave speeches about his life. He often spoke to high school students. He sometimes spoke at as many as five schools during a day. He encouraged the students to achieve their goals.

Kurt received much attention after the 1996 Olympics.

> I was amazed by the sheer athleticism
> of these guys...I thought, why
> couldn't I be a part of this?
> —Kurt Angle, *Salt Lake City Weekly*, 5/10/01

In 1997, Kurt took a job as a weekend sports anchor for a TV station in Pittsburgh. Kurt had no experience in TV news. He made some mistakes on the air. People often made fun of him. Kurt decided he needed to find another job.

WWF Offer

WWF owner Vince McMahon asked Kurt to join the WWF after Kurt won the gold medal. At the time, Kurt had little respect for pro wrestling. Amateur wrestling has stricter rules than pro wrestling has.

Kurt refused McMahon's offer. But in 1998, he started watching the WWF's TV shows. He was impressed with the wrestlers' moves and athletic ability.

A New Career

Kurt changed his mind about McMahon's offer. He called the WWF. But WWF officials were not as interested in Kurt as they had been

WWF official Pat Patterson was impressed with Kurt's athletic ability.

in 1996. Kurt would have to prove his skills before the WWF would hire him.

The WWF brought Kurt to Stamford, Connecticut, to try out. His athletic ability impressed the WWF officials. Kurt had been in Stamford only two days when the WWF asked him to sign a contract.

Kurt wrestled his first match on November 6, 1998, in Salem, Massachusetts. Kurt's

Rival in the Ring: The Rock

Kurt has wrestled all of the top WWF wrestlers. Some of his greatest matches have been against The Rock.

Like Kurt, The Rock is a former football player. He played for the University of Miami in the early 1990s. He is 6 feet, 5 inches (196 centimeters) tall. He weighs 275 pounds (125 kilograms).

The Rock comes from a professional wrestling family. Both his father and grandfather were wrestlers.

In 1996, The Rock joined the WWF as Rocky Maivia. People call him "The People's Champion" and "The Great One." His signature moves are the People's Elbow and the Rock Bottom.

In 2001, The Rock became the first wrestler to win the WWF World Championship six times. He also has won the WCW World Championship twice and the WWF Tag Team Championship five times.

opponent was Dr. Tom Prichard. Kurt won the match.

Joining the WWF

In early 1999, the WWF sent Kurt to wrestle with Power Pro Wrestling in Memphis, Tennessee. By September, he was ready for the WWF. Kurt made his first TV appearance in the WWF on November 14, 1999. He defeated Shawn Stasiak at Survivor Series.

In the ring, professional wrestlers develop a character. Many wrestlers use another name as part of their character. But Kurt uses his own name. He also uses his Olympic gold medal as part of his character. He wears a gold medal into the ring. He always dresses in red, white, and blue.

An Olympic Heel

Some pro wrestlers act mean to other wrestlers or to the fans. These wrestlers are called "heels." Other wrestlers are heroes. They are known as "babyfaces" or "faces."

When Kurt joined the WWF, he was a heel. In the ring, Kurt bragged about his gold medals. He said he was the best wrestler ever. At each match, Kurt insulted the fans. He made fun of their town and the other wrestlers. He acted angry when the fans booed him. He told the fans that they should not boo an Olympic hero. Kurt ended his speeches by saying, "Oh, it's true. It's true."

First Championships

On February 8, 2000, Kurt won his first WWF title. He defeated Sean Morley to win the WWF European Championship. Morley wrestles as Val Venis.

Kurt won his second title less than three weeks later. On February 27, he defeated Chris Irvine to win the WWF Intercontinental Championship. Irvine wrestles as Chris Jericho. Kurt was becoming a WWF star.

WWF Champion

On June 25, 2000, Kurt won the King of the Ring tournament in Boston, Massachusetts. He defeated Rikishi in the final match.

In the ring, Kurt bragged about his gold medals.

Kurt was rising quickly through the WWF. Only one wrestler stood in his way of being at the top. That wrestler was The Rock.

The Rock was the WWF World Champion. In October, Kurt wrestled The Rock for the title at No Mercy. Kurt won the match and the WWF Championship.

Chapter 5

Kurt Angle Today

Kurt successfully defended his World Championship for several months. In February 2001, Kurt lost the title to The Rock at No Way Out in Las Vegas, Nevada.

A New Championship

In March 2001, the WWF bought WCW. About the same time, another wrestling company went out of business. That company was Extreme Championship Wrestling (ECW). Many wrestlers from WCW and ECW came to work for the WWF.

Some WWF fans did not want to watch the new wrestlers. Some of these fans cheered

Kurt often has wrestled The Rock during his WWF career.

for Kurt. Fans liked Kurt because he was a true WWF wrestler. Suddenly, Kurt was a babyface instead of a heel.

On July 24, 2001, Kurt wrestled Booker Huffman for the WCW World Championship. Huffman wrestles as Booker T. The match took place in Pittsburgh. In the past, Pittsburgh fans booed Kurt. But that night, they cheered for him as he defeated Booker T to win the WCW title.

WWF World Champion

Kurt lost the WCW World title to Booker T on July 30. But on September 23, Kurt had another chance to win the WWF World Championship. He returned to Pittsburgh to face Steve Williams at Unforgiven. Williams wrestles as "Stone Cold" Steve Austin.

The night was special to Kurt. His family was there to cheer for him. The Pittsburgh fans also cheered for him. They chanted "Angle" and "U.S.A., U.S.A." during the match.

Kurt began the match by knocking Austin down on the ramp. Austin slammed Kurt into

Kurt wrestled Steve Austin for the WWF World Championship.

the announcer's table three times. Kurt took Austin down with a German suplex. Kurt stood behind Austin. He wrapped his arms around Austin and fell back. Kurt then pulled Austin up and did two more German suplexes.

Later in the match, Kurt used another of his signature moves on Austin. This move is the ankle lock. Austin lay facedown on the mat. Kurt picked up Austin's ankle and twisted it

Kurt's brother Eric (right) also is a professional wrestler.

backward. Austin tapped his arm on the mat in pain. The referee rang the bell. Kurt was again the WWF World Champion.

After the match, Kurt's family ran into the ring to celebrate his win. Kurt rode on his brothers' shoulders as other WWF wrestlers joined them in the ring.

That fall, Kurt won two other titles. On September 10, he defeated Rob Szatkowski to win the WWF Hardcore Championship. Szatkowski wrestles as Rob Van Dam. On October 22, Kurt defeated Terry Gepin to win the WCW U.S. Championship. Gepin wrestles as Rhyno.

Family Life
Kurt's family is very important to him. Kurt met his wife, Karen, after the 1996 Olympics. They married December 19, 1998. Kurt and Karen live in Pittsburgh.

Kurt remains close to his mother, brothers, and sister. Kurt's brother Eric even became a professional wrestler after Kurt joined the WWF. In December 2000, all of Kurt's brothers joined him on a WWF TV show.

Outside the Ring
Kurt has interests other than wrestling. In 2001, he wrote his autobiography. This book about his life is called *It's True! It's True!* Kurt is interested in acting and has taken acting lessons. He has appeared in a few TV commercials and on the game show *The Weakest Link*. Kurt also likes watching sports and playing the drums.

> I didn't know I would have this much passion for this. I have never been more content with what I am doing.
> —Kurt Angle, *Pittsburgh Post-Gazette*, 1/29/01

Kurt stays involved in amateur wrestling. In June 2001, Kurt was named a member of the National Wrestling Hall of Fame. He sometimes works with high school wrestling teams. Kurt says he might coach Olympic wrestlers when his pro wrestling career is over.

Kurt may try out for the 2004 U.S. Olympic wrestling team. He thinks his wrestling skills are still good enough to compete in the Olympics. But he knows he would have to leave pro wrestling for about a year to train for the Olympics.

Kurt also speaks to students. He talks often about his "Three I's." They are intelligence, intensity, and integrity. Kurt says having the Three I's makes him a better person. He tells students to have the Three I's in their lives.

Kurt would like to represent the United States at the 2004 Olympic Games.

Career Highlights

1968—Kurt is born in Pittsburgh, Pennsylvania, on December 9.

1987—Kurt becomes the Pennsylvania state heavyweight wrestling champion.

1987–92—Kurt wrestles at Clarion University in Pennsylvania. He wins two NCAA championships and graduates with a degree in geography.

1996—Kurt wins the Olympic gold medal in the 220-pound (100-kilogram) class in Atlanta, Georgia.

1999—Kurt makes his first WWF TV appearance.

2000—Kurt wins the WWF European Championship, the WWF Intercontinental Championship, the King of the Ring tournament, and the WWF World Championship.

2001—Kurt wins his second WWF World Championship. He also wins the WCW World Championship, WCW U.S. Championship, and WWF Hardcore Championship. Later that year, he publishes his autobiography.

Words to Know

amateur (AM-uh-chur)—an athlete who is not paid for taking part in a sport

autobiography (aw-toh-bye-OG-ruh-fee)—a book in which the author tells the story of his or her life

caution (KAW-shun)—a warning given to amateur wrestlers for breaking a rule during a match

professional (PRUH-fesh-uh-nuhl)—an athlete who is paid to take part in a sport

signature move (SIG-nuh-chur MOOV)—the move for which a wrestler is best known; this move also is called a finishing move.

takedown (TAYK-doun)—an amateur wrestling move that causes the opponent to fall to the mat

tournament (TUR-nuh-muhnt)—a series of contests in which a number of people or teams try to win a championship

To Learn More

Alexander, Kyle. *Pro Wrestling's Most Punishing Finishing Moves.* Pro Wrestling Legends. Philadelphia: Chelsea House, 2001.

Burgan, Michael. *The Rock: Pro Wrestler Rocky Maivia.* Pro Wrestlers. Mankato, Minn.: Capstone High-Interest Books, 2002.

Hunter, Matt. *Superstars of Men's Pro Wrestling.* Male Sports Stars. Philadelphia: Chelsea House, 1998.

Kaelberer, Angie Peterson. *Triple H: Pro Wrestler Hunter Hearst Helmsley.* Pro Wrestlers. Mankato, Minn.: Capstone High-Interest Books, 2003.

Useful Addresses

**National Wrestling Hall of Fame and
  Museum**
405 West Hall of Fame
Stillwater, OK 74075

World Wrestling Entertainment, Inc.
1241 East Main Street
Stamford, CT 06902

Internet Sites

FactHound offers a safe, fun way to find Internet sites related to this book.

Go to www.facthound.com

He'll fetch the best sites for you!

Index